I0440407

SPEED READING FOR ENTREPRENEURS

SEVEN SPEED READING TACTICS TO READ FASTER, IMPROVE MEMORY, AND INCREASE PROFITS

ENTREPRENEUR PUBLISHING

COPYRIGHT

DISCLAIMER

FREE GIFT

Kindle 5 Star Books

Free Kindle 5 Star Book Club Membership

Join Other Kindle 5 Star Members Who Are Getting Private Access To Weekly Free Kindle Book Promotions

Get free Kindle books

Stay connected:

Join our Facebook group

Follow Kindle 5 Star on Twitter

Also, if you want to receive updates on Entrepreneur Publishing's new books, free promotions and Kindle countdown deals sign up to their New Release Mailing List.

For entrepreneurs: http://www.entrepreneurfinesse.com

TABLE OF CONTENTS

Introduction: Why Speed Read?

Tip 1: Choosing Material Selectively

Tip 2: Main Ideas and Summaries

Tip 3: The 80/20 Rule

Tip 4: Increasing Reading Speed

Tip 5: Speed Drills and Why You Should Do Them

Tip 6: Maximizing Retention

Tip 7: Taking Notes: How, When, and Why

Conclusion: Putting It All Together

INTRODUCTION: WHY SPEED READ?

Speed reading is one of those skills that has recently come back in style, thanks in part to a few blogs and training apps dedicated to helping people improve their reading speed and comprehension. It's something that's been touted as an essential skill for decades, and people have been buying in to the idea that you can exponentially increase your reading speed and comprehension since the creation of the concept. While it seems like something that's a gimmick or too good to be true, it's entirely possible and obtainable. You can increase your reading speed and comprehension, and use your new skills to maximize your profits and create more revenue for your business.

So we've gone over the fact that speed reading does, in fact, exist. Great. *But why?* Why should you take time and make the effort (because yes, it will require both time *and* effort) to learn something in addition to the multitude of tasks and challenges you face daily as an entrepreneur? Owning your own business is surely hard enough, and you have plenty of tasks to undertake each day to ensure your business is running smoothly. However there are a few reasons you should undertake speed reading, and a few reasons you can't afford *not* to.

As a small business owner, you're always reading. Whether it's emails, memos, proposals, reports, whatever you have sitting on your desk right now that you're trying to get through in a timely fashion (maybe even this book). Speed reading is going to help you cut down on the time you spend prepping your business, so you can spend more time running it. Speed reading is also good for memory comprehension, so you'll retain more of what you read. As a business owner, your aim is to become the expert in your target area. You want your customers to come to you, and only you, when they need help, and the best way to do so is to educate yourself in your given field as much as possible. Speed reading helps you maximize your productivity, so you can assign more time to doing the tasks that matter the most when improving your small business.

Speed reading is real, has tons of benefits, and it is completely possible to double your reading words per minute (or WPM) with a little time and a lot of effort. It won't happen overnight, but you can learn how to speed read relatively quickly if you follow the seven tips we have outlined for you here.

TIP 1: CHOOSING MATERIAL SELECTIVELY

In order to speed read effectively, there are a few things we need to do before we begin learning the techniques. By doing a little prep work, you can maximize your potential and learn at a steady pace. The faster you master the techniques, the faster you can start doing more for your business to maximize profits.

First, decide what you want to read about. Make a list of a few topics that you plan on becoming more knowledgeable about and why they will be beneficial to your business. If you were having problems getting things done on time, a book or article series on time management would be beneficial. If you're trying to maximize your marketing efforts or looking to cut costs in your advertising, there are a wealth of informative articles and books available to you. Make a list of at least five topics you want to learn about, or areas you want to improve your business.

After making your list, take a good look at what you have written. Some of the subjects, no doubt, will require more research than others, and some subjects will require specific books or technical manuals. You want to make sure when you're reading for entrepreneurial gain, that you're reading the right materials. If you're looking for advice or tips, informal articles and blog posts are all right, but technical knowledge or skills will usually require you to purchase a book.

With your list in sight, try to narrow your search even further. If you're looking to maximize revenue through marketing, try and be specific on what kind of marketing, such as business to business or email marketing. Knowing exactly what you're looking for is key to absorbing quality material. You can read as quickly as you want, but if you're not reading the right thing you won't benefit from any of the material.

Another technique you can employ is to pick reading materials that correspond with the type of materials you are trying to produce. If you're trying to up the number of views you receive on your blog each month, try reading articles and blog posts. If you're looking to write better eBooks, try reading those instead of scanning endless blogs and articles. If it's an actual novel you're looking to write, then you should invest a little time and money into acquiring an actual paperback or hardback copy of a book that you think is relevant to you and your needs. Doing this allows you to look not only the content, but the formatting and vernacular people in your desired field are using to find success. The goal here is to pick your content based on quality not quantity, since this program is designed to make it so you read less overall. The better the information in the first place, the less extra reading you have to do.

An easy way to organize your reading materials is to make piles in order of importance. You can always print blog posts, articles, or emails, so this should not be an issue for you. Print whatever you are wanting to read, and make three piles: Most Important, Moderately Important, Least Important. Reading the most important materials first is vital because your mind is ready to process information at the beginning of your reading session. As you progress, your retention and attention to detail wanes, so you want to make sure the information you get early on is of the most value to you.

Remember, one of the biggest mistakes prospective speed readers make is to try and read as much material as possible once they pick up speed. While you can always read more, the goal is that as a business person you plan on reading less so you can do more, and that means that you need to pick the right quality and the right type of reading material to learn what you need to learn to reach your goals.

TIP 2: MAIN IDEAS AND SUMMARY READING

When you're speed reading, you're looking for the main ideas. The main ideas are the most important part of the piece, and they're what you need to be paying attention to. Much of what you encounter during casual reading is filler material and background details that do not necessarily create the main idea so much as they support it. That's fine, that's how writing should be. However, if you're only willing to invest a small amount of time into reading, you want to get the most out of it that you can.

To read most effectively you, must read actively. An active reader is one who engages with the content versus a passive reader, who just reads to get through the material. Before you begin reading, make a list of questions or objectives you want to accomplish by reading. The prep work you do before you actually begin the reading process is important because it allows you to spend less time on the material overall. By knowing exactly what you're looking for, you can better understand how to get there and where to look for it. Once you have an understanding on what it is you want to accomplish, you can begin using the following techniques to quickly read and glean information from whatever source you plan on using. One of the most effective methods to speed reading is a concept known as main idea and summary reading.

The main idea is often placed in the beginning or at the end of the paragraph. It is the main idea that is sandwiched by details, so you should always start by reading the first and last sentence of any paragraph to learn the summary, or what the entire paragraph is about. The first sentence always introduces the main idea, while the final sentence in the paragraph sums up, and even elaborates on the concept discussed in the paragraph. This is not always the case, but stylistically, most writers put the most vital information at the beginning and end of the paragraph so you can easily understand the flow of information as you read.

After reading that last paragraph, did the main idea concept make sense to you? Go back and re read the first and last sentence only. Together, they read like this: **The main idea is often placed in the beginning or at the end of the paragraph. This is not always the case, but stylistically, most writers put the most vital information at the beginning and end of the paragraph so you can easily understand the flow of information as you read.**

Do you really think you needed to read the entire paragraph in-between to understand the general idea? No, you didn't. The extra details we included between those two sentences only served to support the idea that hey, the important stuff is important. Always remember that the summary is found within the paragraph, and it's usually very obvious to spot.

Another simple tip to maximize your reading will work best if you have an eBook, hard copy book, or anything with an index. Flip to the table of contents page and take a look at a few of the topics. Often, many informative books are not chapter dependent, meaning you are able to skip around to the concepts that interest you, as they do not build on each other as much as you may think. (The exception to this, generally speaking, is text books, and you should really only use this method for an academic or text book setting if you're already familiar with the procedure or material.) Take a moment and consider the table of contents, and only choose to read the section that seems most helpful to you. This is a good method to use if you're picking out a new book or eBook, as it's a good way to get a feel for the type of content and if the quality is there and worthy of your time and money.

If you're reading a blog post or article, there are a few things you can do to make it quicker to understand the main concepts. Blog posts and articles usually have a layout that includes a header and several sub headers, often in a list format. The author does that because readers like their text broken up, and this method is to your benefit. You can scan the article by reading the title and subheadings. If there is a section that interests you, that's when you can begin to scan for the main concepts. Many of these articles include bolded or italicized words, and if they do, you should focus on those sentences or words and their surrounding text the most.

They're highlighted for a reason, and they're designed to catch your attention. Whether the author means to or not, blogs and articles are designed perfectly to help speed readers increase their retention and comprehension.

If you're reading a technical manual, textbook, or other sort of formally created material, you can often check and see if there is a "main concepts" section at the beginning or the end of the section or chapter you're reading. This is especially true with textbooks and manuals, and that area often has the most important information.

These strategies are just a few basic ways to improve your reading speed and retention, but they're not the actual strategy designed to increase your WPM. Before we get into that, you first need to get experience gathering and sorting source material, reading for main concepts and summaries, and understanding the overall meaning of the article without having to read it all. With a little practice, you will master this skill, which will make the remainder of the tips in this eBook easier for you to master. Soon, you'll be reading at speeds you only ever dreamed of.

TIP 3: THE 80/20 RULE

If you've been in the entrepreneurial field for a while, you may have heard of the Pareto Principle, or the 80/20 rule. This rule is a simple way of saying that 80 percent of what you do is a result of 20 percent of your action. A small amount of what you actually do influences a large part of your life. How does this apply to speed reading, though?

To apply the Pareto Principle to speed reading, you have to realize that there is roughly 20 percent of vital material you need to derive from each informative piece you read. Going back to our previous tip on main ideas and summaries, not everything you read is important. And in order to increase your reading speed, you won't be able to actually read everything. Instead, you want to focus your time and energy on fully understanding and comprehending the main ideas, or roughly 20 percent of the stated material.

The texts you read will primarily be on subjects like building your business, increasing your bottom line, time management, and the like. Keep in mind that you don't need to read a wealth of these articles to become knowledgeable. The Pareto principle is founded on minimalism, which embraces the thought of not doing any more work than you absolutely need to to generate the results you want. This applies here too. When building your business, it's important to only spend time with the information that will benefit you. As you go along in your speed reading, you'll learn lots of new information fast. What you need to do is keep track of what information actually *benefits* you overall. So, the email marketing technique you tried didn't work, but you learned quite a bit about time management from the articles you did skim earlier on in the week. That's good, keep track of that. Write it down somewhere, so you know what you're actually learning from. Maybe that time management plan had a useful idea or concept you can apply to managing your staff or creating a new product that will sell itself without needing extensive marketing. Maybe you're inspired to undertake a more vigorous email marketing campaign as a result. This is even better. Keep track of what you gain out of each piece you read so you know where you need to best focus your efforts in the future. Over time, as your reading and comprehension increase you may not have to do this. Maybe you will enjoy doing this so much that you will continue as you learn and gather more information. This is the Pareto Principle as it relates to reading and building your business. By using your source material as informative pieces as much as possible, you eliminate the need to read lots of extra articles that will only tell you the same thing.

To keep the best notes, create a special section in your notebook, binder, or even a spreadsheet on Excel to track the main concepts and actions you take as a result. Print out the source material and write on it, highlight, and create a list of actions you want to take as a result. The more action you take and the more you do as a result of your reading, the less you will have to read. The end goal here in speed reading for entrepreneurs is to eliminate endless hours of poring over articles and break it down into more succinct, easy to understand information that works for you.

Another important aspect of the 80/20 rule is knowing what to let slide. We talked earlier about sorting your material into the Important, Moderately Important, and Not As Important piles. Under the 80/20 rule, you'll be tossing the Not As Important and at least half of your Moderately Important stack in the trash and not looking at them. They're not important overall, and they're not going to help you. The best way to pare down your work load and stay organized is to know when to let go of things. So, as you skim, speed read, and continue to learn and grow, be quick to eliminate any article or piece of material you feel is not going to benefit you. Even if you're already halfway through and it's not doing anything for you, let it go. Don't document it, don't waste time marking up the margins or highlighting the key points. If it's not going to help you, don't let it waste your time.

The 80/20 rule focuses on productivity, or getting the most done in the shortest amount of time. To do this, take a few minutes and consider when you are most productive. Are you an early morning person that likes to get stuff done and out of the way immediately? Or do you find yourself more of a night owl that gets the most accomplished when the sun goes down? As an entrepreneur you probably have a full schedule, and that's okay, but when it comes to reading and learning, you need to make sure to carve out an appropriate niche of time you can dedicate to the task, ideally when you are at your most productive. Create a time, say half an hour a day, and conduct your research and reading in a tranquil environment conducive to study so you can get the most done.

These are just a few ways the Pareto principle is important in helping you gain success with speed reading, and we want you to keep the ideas and concepts in mind as we progress further. The next several tips are going to include practical applications and drills that you will use to help increase your reading speed and comprehension, so it's important to understand the general concepts before we get into the complicated stuff.

Tip 4: Increasing Reading Speed

Believe it or not, there is a reason you read at a certain pace. Whether you are aware of it or not, you're probably reading this book out loud in your head. This is called sub vocalization, and it is the reason we are only able to read at a specific pace. There's no coincidence you can only read as fast as you can speak; as a child, you learn speech and vocabulary before you learn how to read and write, so your brain takes the words on a page and translates them to the vocals you are familiar with. The average person reads between 150 and 250 words per minute, which is also the average talking speed. No coincidence there. Sub vocalization dramatically diminishes the amount of text you can read and comprehend in a short period of time. However, there are a few things you can do that will increase your overall reading speed. These are some good ways to speed read if you are not a fan of scanning text or if you feel the article has too many important points to cover with the methods listed above.

Using your finger as a guide is one of the most effective ways to eliminate sub vocalization and read faster. Your eye focuses on moving objects, and when it comes to text it processes the text in a series of chunks before moving on the next segment. To test this theory, place your finger lightly on top of your eyelid as you read the rest of this paragraph. As you read, you should feel a very subtle movement every several words on the eyelid. This is your eye's way of refocusing, and it is another contributing factor to your reading speed. The best way to eliminate this is to eliminate the way your eyes fixate on words, and using your pointer finger as a guide is the best way to do that.

Take your pointer finger and run it across the length of the sentence in the article or book you are trying to read. Your eyes follow your finger instead of their normal fixation pattern, and you are able to get through a line of text up to 25 percent faster than you would otherwise. If you're wondering if this technique really is an effective way to increase your reading speed, try reading the last few paragraphs over again, timed, without your finger. Then, do the same reading with your pointer finger as a guide, and compare the two. Chances are, your second time is marginally faster than the first. This is a good trick to use when reading longer manuals that you find cumbersome or hard to focus on, as it forces your eyes and brain to pay attention.

Using your environment is another good way to increase your overall reading speed. The goal of using your environment is to reduce sub vocalization, so you can begin reading faster. The first thing you want to do is to ensure, of course, that you are in an environment that is conducive to learning and reading. A home office, desk, or kitchen table free of other extraneous distractions is essential, and it's also important that you take up reading at the same time each day. We want to create one habit (speed reading) while breaking another (sub vocalization), and repetition is the most important way to do both.

Once you have your space picked out, pick up your headphones. Turning on music is a good way to distract your brain and allow you to focus on the words as they are without being able to read them mentally. Be careful here: not all types of music will help you when it comes to improving your reading speed. You want to pick something that doesn't have really strong vocals or a big beat, but is more relaxing and calm. Something like soft rock, classical, jazz, or even opera is always a safe bet because they are enjoyable without being too distracting. It's also important to note that you shouldn't turn your headphones or stereo system up too loud, as the music volume can actually be just as distracting as regular music would be.

Another trick is to occupy your mouth while you are reading. Many people read under their breath, or use their mouth to form the words they are reading on the page. This sub vocalization technique is easy to spot, and if it is a habit of yours, very difficult to break. One of the easiest ways to distract yourself from speaking the words as you read is to chew a piece of gum or candy. Some speed readers even report getting a lot of their reading done during mealtimes, because the constant chewing of food is a great distraction from reading the words out loud (and let's face it, it's also a pretty great way to multitask).

If you're reading some text online, there is a great application you can use to help you increase your reading speed. Accelareader.com is a website dedicated to helping people increase their reading speeds, and it's a fun tool to use if you're just starting out and trying to increase your speed to 300 words per minute or higher. All you have to do is copy the text you want to read, and paste it into the reader on the website. Then, pick how fast you want to read, and the words blink across the screen at the desired speed. This is also a great way to help train your eyes to stop fixating on words for too long, as a big portion of reading speed involves rereading and fixating on one word. Remember that the faster you go, the less words you'll vocalize in your head each time.

Another way to increase your overall reading speed is to occupy your sub vocalizing voice with a different task. You can count "1, 2, 3" in your head, while fixating your eyes on the beginning, middle, and end of the line of text as you do so. This is important because we mentioned earlier on in the tip that your eyes take in sections of text at a time and then move on to the next, and the best way to work with this natural eye movement is to employ this technique. You're just retraining your eyes to focus on the text in different sections than they were previous. It is also a good technique to help you pick out the important parts of each sentence, and then put them together for maximum comprehension. Try this next time you are trying to increase your reading speed, and you will probably be surprised at how easy it is to read faster.

Perhaps the most simple way to speed read is just to make yourself read faster. If you measure the words per minute that you normally read, you can push for reading a little bit more in the same amount of time. Say you read 200 words per minute. That's a fair, average number, but you are hoping to read at least 300 words per minute. If you do some drills for speed (we'll talk about some speed drills you can do in the next tip), then you can definitely increase your reading speed. Simply by being aware of the fact that you're trying to read faster will often reduce sub vocalization because your eyes are seeing the words faster. This is a simple technique, but you won't believe how many people do not think to employ it in the hopes of reading a little faster.

The goal of speed reading is not to completely eliminate sub vocalization, we want to make that very clear. While a lot of speed reading programs out there will try and tell you that you need to completely eliminate it for your reading speed to increase, you don't have to eliminate it in its entirety to read faster and comprehend more. Truly what you have to do is read with more purpose and more awareness than you have in the past. By doing this, you'll increase your reading speed, retention, and knowledge base with ease.

Tip 5: Speed Drills And Why You Should Do Them

This next tip focuses on speed drills. A lot of speed readers like to skip over speed drills because they do not see the merit in trying to read the same thing over and over. While that's fair, it's important to remember that reading is a lot like running: you have to practice to get better. You probably read much, much faster than you did when you were first learning words, and just like a runner in the Boston Marathon runs much faster than he or she did when he or she first ran a 5k race. This is the same thing. It is going to take a little bit of time and effort on your part initially, but if you're willing to put in a little work with the following speed drills, then you will see the benefits in how quickly you're able to pick up speed.

The first speed reading drill employs something called The Deadline Technique. This is a very simple drill that is designed to measure how fast you can read a page of text. Take a page of text (maybe the 10th page of this eBook, for example) and set a timer on your phone or stopwatch. Using your normal reading techniques, read the page and record your time. This will be your benchmark. Next, you want to read another page of different text using the speed reading tips you have picked up so far in this book. Time yourself and record your time. Now, you will use that as your bench mark and begin practicing to read faster. Skim another page for main ideas, and see how long it takes you to get through that page with your timer. After using the Deadline Technique, you will understand how important awareness is when you're reading. This helps to enforce the idea of Active Reading, or reading with a purpose. Use this as a tool to track your progress as you continue to improve in your techniques.

This next speed reading drill is not necessarily a drill in the sense of the word so much as it is an exercise. For this exercise, you will want to pick a book you have read before, preferably something you enjoyed enough the first time to read again. As you read, take note of how your brain picks up on the words. You already know the main characters, the plot, the rising and falling action, the outcome, all of the minor nuances in the book. Chances are if it took you say, six hours to read the book the first time, it will take you significantly less to read it a second time. This is because your brain is picking up on the important bits of information, and you are subconsciously scanning past anything you already know is unnecessary to the outcome of the book. This is a great way to train your brain to understand information and process it faster. Not everything you read is important. If you're reading for leisure (in this instance, and for the purpose of this eBook, you are not), then it is more than alright to take your time and get to know a book, but here you want to get as much information in a short time. Fixation and rereading are big deal breakers when it comes to reading speed; they're the reason we often take longer than we would like to finish a novel or technical manual. However, even though you have already read the material previously, you are still training your mind to treat new material the same way, by picking out the important information and leaving the filler out.

An added benefit to this exercise is that you get to enjoy a piece of literature all over again. If you do not want to read a novel, you can always go for a technical manual or training guide for something. Books like that tend to need to be read more than once for comprehension as it is, so maybe you will gain extra knowledge as a result.

Another speed reading drill that acts more as an exercise is to test your focus and comprehension as you read. Taking breaks is essential to speed reading, because it allows your brain to process information (we'll talk more on comprehension and memory in the next tip). Without focus, what you read is no longer relevant, as you will not stand to gain any valuable information from it. Instead, try reading and taking short breaks. For every ten minutes you read, take a sixty second break to write down notes, rest your eyes, or take a breather. Because you are trying to maximize on your time, it is a good idea to use this time to jot down a few notes (again, we will discuss note taking in tip seven), collect your thoughts, and most importantly, determine if the information you're reading is still worthy of your time. Many articles and books have a few important things that you need to be aware of, and the rest is just fluff. If you are starting to think that the piece you are reading is becoming less relevant, stop reading immediately and move on to something else. Not everything is important, and this will increase your speed all the more because by switching papers or taking breaks, you are refreshing your brain and eyes so they will behave as if you are just starting to read.

Keep in mind that these speed reading drills and exercises are just that: exercises. The most important part of succeeding at any task is repetition and perseverance, and you will need to keep this in mind when you're beginning your drills. If you are really wanting to get better and improve your speed and comprehension, you will if you follow the exercises and keep at it. Everybody learns at a different pace, and you will learn the best at the pace that is right for you. Just be diligent, set aside the appropriate amount of time based on your schedule, and create a game plan for what you want to know and how you want to learn about it. It will seem like a little more prep work initially, but as you grow and improve with the program, you will be amazed at what you get accomplished.

TIP 6: MAXIMIZING RETENTION AND COMPREHENSION

You can be the fastest reader in the world. No really, you can. Wouldn't that be amazing, to read whatever you want in the blink of an eye? Sure, but what if you were unable to recall any of that information? Now, that sounds like a pretty raw deal, doesn't it? If you don't understand and remember what you have read, then the whole process is pointless. No matter how fast you read, you have to be able to understand the material, relate to it, and remember it for later on. As an entrepreneur, the things you learn have to be turned into strategies to grow your business and increase your profits, and you can't hope to do that if you are unable to remember the revolutionary tips you have read or the awesome advice you have stashed away from the last book you perused. Basically, there are a few ways you can maximize your comprehension, or understanding, and retention, or memory for later on.

The first way to maximize comprehension is to take notes. We will get more in depth on how to take notes in the next tip, but the goal of note taking in speed reading is that you are able to recall more information after you are finished without having to consult the source material for clarification. Rereading and fixating on certain aspects of the text are some of the main reasons it takes us so long to get though lengthy articles or books, and by taking notes you eliminate the need to go dig the book back out, turn to the specific chapter, and reread or scan everything until you find the section that is relevant to you. And then, you may not have all of the information you need to move on because you have more information to find. And thus, the cycle continues and you are stuck digging through your print outs, books, and manuals as if you had never read them in the first place. Instead, take notes as you go along, and keep them organized. Tip seven is full of great ways to take notes and how to keep them organized, so read to that section for more elaborate information.

As you go along, it is important for your comprehension and memory to stop reading. Taking breaks is so important because it allows your brain to digest information and reflect before moving on to the next snippet. This leads to increased comprehension and increased memory overall. Even if you do not plan on taking notes, it is still vital that you step away from the material for a few minutes at staged intervals to allow your brain a rest. It is recommended that you take a five minute break for every fifteen minutes you read, or a twenty minute break every hour. It is generally recommended that you take no more than a half hour break between lengthy (one hour or more) sessions so that you do not end up losing any of that information. If you are reading or working on a tablet, computer, phone, or other electronic device, it is heavily advised that you take more frequent breaks. For your optical health, eye care professionals recommend frequent, shorter breaks as your eyes can become fatigued from staring at high contrast screens for extended lengths of time. If you are reading printed source material, it is still a good idea to give your eyes and mind a quick interlude. Not only will you reduce the number of headaches you get, you will also have more energy and the ability to speed read for longer periods of time while still maintaining memory and comprehension.

Another great way to up your comprehension and memory when speed reading is to rehearse what you have just read. It may sound silly, but many professionals swear by this method because it actually forces you to engage with the material in a dynamic way. After reading a chapter or section, jotting down some notes, and getting a full grasp of the concepts, take a few minutes to break and begin rehearsing what you have just read. A good strategy to employ is to recite it in a short speech format, as if you were telling a friend or family member about this concept and he or she had absolutely no idea what it was or why it would help you. Along with this, be sure to talk about how this concept or this section will help you grow your business. "These time management strategies will help me cut overhead costs because I will be making less mistakes and creating product with more efficiency than I am currently." Something like that actually forces you to examine what you're reading, and determine if it will work for you. Again, if you are trying to answer your questions from earlier and you feel like the information fails to help, then you have to get rid of it.

Reading at your peak time is also another great way to maximize retention. If you're an early morning type of person, try and get your learning done early on in the day. If you work best when the sun is down, then set aside some time at night to do some speed reading and learning. It is always best to do things when you are at your most productive and when your brain is most alert. Make sure the place you are working is a good, stable environment, such as a home office. We know we've mentioned this before, but we cannot stress enough the importance of a good space, especially in the hectic world of an entrepreneur. The ideal space should be where you find yourself to be the most productive. Maybe you love going to your local Starbucks and working on a project. If you do, that's more than all right. Just go down and have a seat and get to work. Wherever you feel comfortable is where you should be.

Drinking a caffeinated drink is another interesting tip for memory retention, and we figured it may help some if we included it here. Johns Hopkins has conducted studies on caffeine and memory retention and has found that caffeine has a positive effect on long-term memory and can lead to greater memory retention over time. So have a cup of coffee or your favorite tea as you are reading. It's a great way to distract your mouth (remember sub vocalization), and it's also a great way to perk up your brain and help you remember some of the more important key concepts. Obviously, if you are caffeine sensitive or do not wish to partake, please refrain from doing so and know your limits if you do, but it is an interesting experiment and may appeal to those of us busy men and women that can't get on without our coffee in the morning.

Another key method to comprehension that many people do not think about is using the tools at your disposal. The Internet is full of summaries, synopses, and informative videos that can help you when you are getting ready to read source material. Even Wikipedia, for all of its dubious formatting and ambiguous editing practices, can be useful when looking for big picture ideas and helping you remember what you have read. If you are looking into a book, read a synopsis or summary online and use that as a way to speed read. You'll remember more and understand the big picture if it is laid out for you clearly.

You can speed read videos, emails, memos, and anything else of the like as well. Just make sure you are breaking these things up into sections, taking breaks, rehearsing what you have just learned, and keeping your notes thorough and up to date and you won't have any problem using alternative source material as a way to help you out.

TIP 7: TAKING NOTES: HOW, WHEN, AND WHY

Taking notes is an important and vital part of your speed reading process. You absolutely have to take notes when you're reading, because they will save you time and effort when you want to go about creating a plan and implementing it. If you do not take notes, you may find yourself having to search through your source material all over again to find information you previously read. While this is not a necessarily catastrophic occurrence, especially if your reading speed has improved, it is still so important that you actually have something you can look back on outside of your source material. There are a few important methods and reasons you should take notes, and we aim to tell you exactly how and when you should expect to do so for the best retention and results.

When taking notes, it is best if you do so as you are reading the material, instead of going back at the end to gather your thoughts. While reflection is important after you are finished reading, it is also important that you do not reread and fixate on text (remember how we mentioned how that increased your reading time earlier?). The best way to take notes is to break your material up into sections. Many articles will be sectioned off into bullet points or paragraphs, and books may be sectioned off into chapters, but you can also break them down further if you would like. After reading and skimming each section, write down what is most important. Write down key words, main concepts, and anything else you found noteworthy in the text. Often, you will encounter sections that are not as important as you initially thought, and that is more than all right. Just skip that section and move on to something else. It is best not to linger on any one section too long, but to keep going and working toward the end of the piece.

One of the biggest problems with taking notes is that people actually take too many of them! Believe it or not, you are probably more verbose in your notes than you need to be, and there are plenty of strategies to help you eliminate excess baggage from your notebooks. Keep in mind that note taking is part of your speed reading process, so you will have to factor that in as part of your overall time and try and speed this process up as well.

Abbreviation is an important part of note taking that will save you time in the long run when it comes to looking back on your notes. Abbreviations are always different based on who writes them, but make sure it is something you can understand later on. Many people will write out the first few letters and then abbreviate with a period to convey the abbreviation. (An example of this would be envel. instead of envelope.) You can also abbreviate by just using a few key letters (typwr instead of typewriter, for example), but keep them in the same order as they are spelled. Remember that this is just one aspect of note taking, and that to successfully shave time off of it, you need to employ a few other strategies as well

Another great thing you can do to create better notes is to annotate the source material as you read. This is something many high school and post secondary educators teach their students, because it allows their students to study the material and remember everything much better than they would otherwise. The first thing you want to do is print out your source material. Articles and blog posts you can definitely print with ease. eBooks (depending on their size, of course) are also able to be printed, and books and text books should be your own personal copies if you plan on annotating them (if they are not, you can always make photocopies and keep them for personal use). After printing out your source material, grab a pen and a highlighter. Now, begin speed reading. For note taking purposes, you usually want to use the first methods of skimming for comprehension and reading the main ideas. If you see any words that are unfamiliar or seem like key words, highlight them right there on the page. Off to the side, make sure to write the main idea of each paragraph. After each section or chapter, write a one or two sentence summary of what you learned and what the main ideas are. Having the information right on the actual source material is definitely helpful when you are trying to compile a list of answers to your questions, and remember what you have learned.

Another powerful note taking tool is called mind mapping. Mind mapping is great for comprehension as well as note taking, because it allows you to organize everything in an easy to see, easy to read visual format. If you are a visual learner or you just really like graphs, you will enjoy using the mind mapping process as you speed read. First, read the section as you would, implementing the speed reading techniques you have already been mastering. Then, once you have the feel for the main idea of a piece, get out a blank sheet of paper and write it down in the middle. Nothing elaborate, just a few words or a phrase that tells you what you are reading about.

After you do that, begin reading again. As you pause to take notes, start writing down ideas, key phrases, and other important bits of information that you are gleaning from the text. Create little bubbles for them, and link them back to the main idea. You can also link them to each other, as more details come about and more concepts and main ideas begin interlocking to form a bigger understanding. Mind mapping is a lot like brainstorming in that it helps you understand a lot with visual cues, so when you look back on your notes you can see how the information relates from one concept to the next and how they are all relevant when looking at the main idea. This is also a great comprehension exercise, especially if you are reading something that builds on itself, like a textbook or technical manual. Keep in mind that this is like traditional liner note taking and that you need to be purposeful with the things you put in your mind map. Do not include unnecessary details, and be careful to not add too much. With a little practice, your mind maps will help pave the way for better and more conclusive note taking.

If you do not like the idea of mind mapping, you can also create a separate notebook for all of your notes and information. In fact, we recommend it. Annotating and mind mapping are great, but any good business person knows that there is value in having all of your thoughts organized and in a concise place. It is very important with note taking too that you create an organizational system and then stick to it. When you start to learn more and more about your subject your notes can become more and more elaborate and lengthy without you meaning for it to happen, and that is not a bad thing. Instead, you need to periodically go through and prune the things that are not relevant to what you're trying to accomplish.

And perhaps the most important part about note taking is to actually make sure the notes you are taking will help you. You can take the best notes in the world and they will do you little good if they are not helping you answer your questions. Remember how we mentioned posing a few questions or things you wanted to learn more about as part of your reading prep work? Keep those typed or written out somewhere, and take a careful look at your notes.

"What is answering this question? What has little relevance here? Is there something I may be missing, or an area I have not explored yet? And how can I take my source material and concepts and apply them to various aspects of my learning?" These are some questions you need to ask yourself as you take notes and as you begin to organize and reread over what you have written down. The bottom line is that if it does nothing to answer a question or enhance your knowledge in the direction you wanted to go initially, it goes in the trash can and you forget about it. We've said it before and we will say it again: not all of what you read is important, and not all of it is worth your time.

CONCLUSION

Speed reading is a valuable skill that anybody, no matter what industry you work in, can benefit from. As an entrepreneur, it is vital that you learn the most information possible in order to maximize profits, increase your bottom line, and allow your business to grow and flourish the proper way. So many people think speed reading is a gimmick or something that you need special training for, and while training programs do exist, they are not always necessary to creating a skill that will serve you well in the long run.

For a small business owner, you want to make sure that the quality of the material you plan on reading is the best you can find. Scour Internet sources, books, articles, and journals for the highest quality publications you can acquire. If you're working in a specific medium (such as blogging or writing books), then look for material in those specific formats so you can understand what success in those industries looks like. The better quality the material, the better your results will be.

Knowing what you want to learn and what you plan on doing with the information you obtain is so vital in speed reading success. If you don't know the question, you simply cannot expect to obtain the answer with any sort of ease. Write down a few questions, ideas, or things you want to know and learn, and use this as a sort of benchmark when doing your research into your source materials.

Scanning for main ideas and summaries dramatically reduce your reading time, and increase your overall comprehension of the material. Not everything you read is important, and not everything out there is worth your time and energy. Instead, focus on finding four or five premium sources and using those as a guide to help you grow your business.

Speed drills are another important way to increase your reading comprehension. Many speed reading professionals suggest using a pen, your hand, or some sort of object to allow the eye to move more fluidly from the beginning of a line of text to the end. This is so important because increasing reading speed is the result of reduction of sub vocalization, or the internal voice in your head that reads the words at the same rate you talk. It is a completely natural phenomenon, but that is one of the main things that holds people back when it comes to speed reading.

Don't forget that it's not enough to just read something, you must also comprehend what you read, and remember the information to recall it later. Do a few memory drills, write things, down, and make sure that you keep your thoughts and ideas organized when it comes to reflecting on your reading and what you have learned.

Notes, notes notes! Another important part of speed reading for entrepreneurs is note taking. So many people forget to do this, or are simply too lazy, that it no wonder some people have such a hard time with speed reading. Taking notes not only helps you increase your comprehension and memory retention, it also helps you for when you want to go back over the material later on. You will find it unnecessary to open your files up, locate the article, and scan over it until you find the specific part if you create detailed notes on all of the important concepts you have learned while reading. This is how speed reading really differs from reading for fun, in that it requires extra work besides the actual reading in order to really obtain something of value.

As you can probably see from everything you have read, speed reading for entrepreneurs takes a little more work than simply reading a chunk of text. While it's true that speed reading is something that is completely obtainable, you have to remember that it is going to take a little time and effort to get started. We cannot stress enough how important practice and perseverance are when you're doing your drills or scanning documents for information. It may feel weird or not entirely natural to not just read the text as intended to be read, but you will be shocked at how quickly you adapt to the process.

Above all else, just give the process a chance. Stay away from feelings of doubt or worry about the challenge that speed reading provides. It seems like something that's really tough, but in reality it's not nearly as difficult as many professionals and speed reading course salespeople make it out to be. You can always purchase a speed reading course, but your best bet is to take the tips in this eBook and start applying them each day. Carve out a section of time where you can really dedicate yourself to improvement, and we promise that you'll be amazed at your results. We hope this book helped you learn and understand a little more about speed reading, and all of the wonderful things it can do for you and for your business. Good luck on this and all of your future endeavors, from everyone here at Entrepreneur Publishing.

To hear about Entrepreneur Publishing's new books first (and to be notified when there are free promotions), sign up to their New Release Mailing List.

Finally, if you enjoyed this book, please take the time to share your thoughts and post a review on Amazon. It'd be greatly appreciated!

Thank you and good luck!

Preview Of 'Gardening For Entrepreneurs: Gardening Techniques For High Yield, High Profit Crops' from Entrepreneur Publishing

Marketing Tips and Strategies for Your Growing Enterprise

In most cases, the amount of profit your growing enterprise can generate will come down to two factors; the quality of your produce and how you market it. With earnings per acre varying from $2,000 to $20,000 for a year, this type of venture can provide a serious income and a long-term enterprise. However, while you may be able to sell lower quality produce with fantastic marketing skills, if your marketing techniques are lacking, you are likely to struggle to sell even the most amazing produce. This means that learning some new marketing skills to sell your crops should be a priority. Fortunately, there are a number of strategies, which can help you and may influence the type of crops you wish to grow.

Essential Factors for Easier Marketing:

The techniques for selling your produce can vary and some growers will often use a number of methods simultaneously for optimum results. However, regardless of your marketing approach, there are several factors that you will need to consider.

Quality:

The first of these considerations is the quality of your product. You may be the type of salesperson who can sell sand in the desert, but having a good quality product makes sales far easier. You need to ensure that you produce the best possible product, Your produce should look healthy and clean to appeal to potential buyers. Sub-standard produce is far harder to sell and will group you with "ordinary" produce available at the local branch of a grocery store chain. This means that you will need to follow the planning, preparation and techniques detailed earlier in this book to produce the highest possible quality.

You will also want to take proactive action to eliminate any pests which could damage your plants and produce. This could include using natural pest repellents such as basil, garlic, thyme, catnip, marigolds and tansy or learning organic pest treatments such as orange oil. Part of your marketing strategy will need to be dedicated to research, from looking at customer demand through to learning accepted growing methods and techniques. This will make your overall marketing easier as you can have confidence in the quality of your product.

Timing:

Another important consideration for your marketing strategy is your timing. If you are able to produce a crop when other producers are still waiting to harvest, obtaining sales can be easy. This could involve using greenhouses, extending your growing season and planting early. You don't want to be late to the party on a time sensitive crop. For example, Brussels sprout growers are going to be out of luck if their crop is only ready to be harvested on December 26th. Therefore, you need to plan your crop properly to ensure that it is ready when you need it to get those sales.

Pricing:

The price at which you market your produce is also an important factor. Most growers will price their produce at up to twenty percent less than grocery stores. However, don't attempt to undercut the price of other small producers, as you may end up locked into a pricing war. Organic produce will automatically command a premium price, so compare local retail stores, other sellers and farmers markets to check out the current local selling rate.

Selling to a Specific Market:

Once you are confident of your quality, timing and price, you will need to get your produce to potential customers. This can be accomplished in a number of ways depending on your target market.

Selling Direct to the Public:

The most common technique to market your produce is selling your products at a roadside stand. However, before you consider this technique you should consider whether there is ample parking space and that you have adequate signage. Your signs need to be placed far enough away from the actual stand to allow drivers time to slow down and pull in. The signs should be clear and easy to understand with no more than seven or eight words. Don't make the sign so bright that it isn't legible and keep it looking professional.

You will need to organize your stand so that it has a neat appearance. Customers should be able to see the produce and prices easily. This care and attention is sure to pay off when combined with good prices and quality produce as "word of mouth" will provide a great deal of free advertising. If you don't want to invest in a stand initially, the same technique can be applied if you sell from the back of your car or pickup truck.

Another approach to sell your products is a farmer's market. Most areas have a schedule of regular farmer's markets to allow you to sell your organic produce. If your area does not have a market, you may wish to invest the time with other producers in your area to organize one.

The pick your own strategy is also another excellent method of marketing directly to the public. You can advertise in local newspapers, bulletin boards, community newsletters and websites. Don't forget to put up signage for your plot and plan out plenty of parking and customer amenities such as temporary toilets. Many of your potential customers will view a pick your own plot as a family event, so be prepared for small children to arrive with their parents by ensuring the site is safe from any hazardous tools and materials. You may wish to implement certain rules about small children if you are concerned about damage to crops or potential injury. Be aware that adverse weather will mean that your customers will not want to spend time outside picking, so be sure to advertise that you also sell by the container on site.

A successful pick your own venture requires you to have great people skills, as every visitor needs to be treated as an important customer. One aspect of a pick your own operation, you will need to accept as a cost of doing business, is that a large percentage of your customers will be sampling the merchandise. Children especially will be prone to popping fruit in their mouth rather than the container. This should be viewed as a good-natured goodwill gesture unless it becomes particularly problematic. Some humorous signs informing customers that fruit should go in the container, not the mouth, will usually do the trick.

Selling to Restaurants:

Restaurant management and chefs are always in need of good quality produce. If you are able to provide restaurants with steady supplies of fresh organic produce, you are likely to find plenty of customers. When considering selling to restaurants, seeing is believing. While some restaurants will discuss potential purchases over the phone, often showing the quality of your produce is a more effective marketing approach. Don't visit the restaurant during lunch or dinner service, but rather go when they have time to speak to you and check out what you have to offer. You are likely to need to give some assurances about the frequency and volume of produce before restaurants will switch suppliers, but if you can offer a discount and high quality produce, most will give you a try. Be sure to nurture these relationships and deliver as agreed for long-term profits and success.

Selling to Retailers:

Selling your produce to retailers can be another excellent way to market your venture. When you contact stores and retailers, you will need to be prepared to offer a discount of up to forty percent from the typical retail prices. This will create an attractive profit margin for most stores. If you can demonstrate reliability, you may be able to offer a weekly route between a number of retail locations. If your harvest is likely to provide a more bulk amount of produce, you could consider a food co-op.

Co-ops are more able and eager to consider a large quantity of good quality produce. You will need to be prepared to offer a reasonable discount to attract interest. Most co-ops will require you to contact them directly and you may need to prepare packages of your produce rather than a bulk load. For example, herbs are more attractive in one or two ounce labeled bags.

Internet Sales:

For most modern day entrepreneurs, the Internet provides a great marketplace and for certain types of gardening can offer a great sales opportunity. If you are selling specialist items, which have a national demand, you could market your items online. For example, there are a number of growers offering unusual types of mushrooms by next day mail order online. Many consumers will pay a premium for this convenience, especially if the item is not available for them locally. This is obviously not practical for larger vegetable items, which are readily available in most areas. Additionally, although there are next day courier services available, the appeal of most of your produce will be that it is local and fresh.

However, if you are planning on selling dried items such as flowers or herbs, there could be an online demand for your items, in fact certain specialist items have a greater demand for dried products such as mushrooms. Therefore, you may find it more profitable to dry your mushrooms and offer them for sale nationally rather than selling them fresh locally.

Selling a Finished Product:

Another marketplace for your items could be selling a finished product to the public or to retailers. For example, you could create a range of baked goods made using your organic produce. This is a more intensive enterprise and would be subject to more rigorous local and state laws. However, there have been a number of brands, which have emerged from a small enterprise making cakes, muffins, cookies or baby food with organic fresh produce. This can be especially profitable if you are able to appeal to a niche market such as vegetarians or vegans, dieters or the health conscious. Other entrepreneurs have developed full businesses based on their own organic produce. For example, if you have always dreamed of owning your own restaurant or cafe, your fresh organic produce could provide the cornerstone of your appeal.

Click here to check out the rest of Gardening For Entrepreneurs: Gardening Techniques For High Yield, High Profit Crops on Amazon.

Or go to: http://amzn.to/1CpHHDX

MORE BOOKS FOR ENTREPRENEURS

Click here to check out the rest of Entrepreneur Publishing's books on Amazon.

Below you'll find some of my other popular books that are popular on Amazon and Kindle as well. Simply click on the links below to check them out. Alternatively, you can visit my author page on Amazon to see other work done by me.

How Audiobooks Make You Smarter: 7 Little Known Ways Audio Books Can Boost Memory Capacity And Increase Intelligence

How To Write A Book And Publish On Amazon: Make Money With Amazon Kindle, CreateSpace And Audiobooks

Gardening For Entrepreneurs: Gardening Techniques For High Yield, High Profit Crops

Speed Reading For Entrepreneurs: Seven Speed Reading Tactics To Read Faster, Improve Memory And Increase Profits

Content Marketing Strategies: How Delivering Sensational Value Can Help You Build A Digital Media Empire

If the links do not work, for whatever reason, you can simply search for these titles on the Amazon website to find them.

www.ingramcontent.com/pod-product-compliance
Lightning Source LLC
Chambersburg PA
CBHW071349310526
45790CB00018B/1402